Time Lapse Mosaic

Anne Beck

BookLeaf Publishing

Presentation by *BookLeaf Publishing*

Web: www.bookleafpub.com

E-mail: info@bookleafpub.com

ISBN: 9789357211994

First edition 2023

DEDICATION

With much love and thanks to Maria, who encouraged my first poetic endeavors and supported so much of my growth over these years.

ACKNOWLEDGEMENT

With gratitude to the inspiration of Book Leaf Publishing's November 2022 #TheWriteAngle Challenge, without which this book would not yet have become a reality.

PREFACE

This is a book of poetry - poems that span the work of over ten years of writing, and poems that are the result of a recently renewed effort to invest more in creative writing. Most of them are unpublished until now. They offer a glimpse into Anne's creative mind and her poetic vision of the world. To her, poems are paintings made with words. They are not meant to be perfect. They are at times overflowing with wonder and joy, and at times clumsy attempts to touch some mysterious paradox or question. She hopes they might touch you too.

Imagination

An arch not of stone,
A road without end,
A whirl of blue
  In an infinite sky;

A door with no latch,
A way into worlds,
A window that lacks
  Both a frame and glass panes;

A house with no roof
  Under a sea full of stars;

The doorstep to nowhere
  Is the threshold of anywhere.

Wind-Waves and Stars

Late in the night when the wind is high,
And the middle of summer is drawing nigh,
Then we shall visit the starry sea
And hearken to tide of wind in tree.

The swift cloud-boats go sailing on
Forever until the tide is gone,
And bright star-fishes look twinklingly
From the darkening depths of the floor of the sea.

The wind-waves rise with a measured roar,
On coral reefs break, and are heard no more;
They murmur and sigh among leaf-coral green,
Then rise and curl again unseen.

We'll take for a boat the crescent-shaped moon;
With a moonbeam we'll go star-fishing soon,
Where the waking world meats the dreamy sea
In the wind-swept deeps of a star-filled sea.

The End of Autumn

When winds of November begin to bite,
And frost settles down on the hills at night;
The geese from the north come southward flying;
Their plaintive calls ring crying, crying:
Farewell to the corn-fields cut and dried
  That quietly wait for the falling snow,
Gleaned by the geese from far and wide
  That noisily on their way now go.

Warm though the rays of the autumn sun,
Crisp is the air when the day is done;
An arrow against the sunset, winging
Their way to the south and singing, singing:
Farewell to the maples red and gold,
  The oaks and the elms full of autumn fire;
The geese travel on when the year grows old,
  When wind-tossed leaves set the earth on fire.

Swift runs the deer through the bare brown brush;
The river sweeps by in a last great rush;
The geese have all gone, and the light is dying;
Brown fall the leaves now, sighing, sighing:
Farewell to the splendor of the year's last days,
  For autumnal glory has come and gone;
The world will to sleep while Jack Frost plays,
  And wake from the dead at the break of dawn.

Time's Travels

When the sun has set amid splendorous rays,
Of gold and grander hues, glowing like fire,
And dusk has dropped its dew down to the earth,
The moonlight mingles with the midnight stars,
The stars that trek a silent course slowly across the sky.
They travel with Time as he treads the path
Of minutes that make a month or many a year.
As this wayfarer wends the winding way to his end
He roams without rest, and returns not ever,
For the past is past and the present a moment,
And the future not fixed in the frame of Time's folly.
Yet he never hastens or hurries, nor holds back either,
Although in our thoughts we may think that he does;
He watches the world a-wandering in war and peace
and might.
He bears the balance on
Of Nature's day and night;
The dawning day upon
The horizon beams now bright.

Arbor Unicornis

In the midst of a forest
Beneath a great oak tree
Stood a little and lone unicorn.

The storm-winds came howling
And shaking the forest
But the oak stood unbending and calm.

'Twas a pillar of strength
And a haven of silence
And the magic that moved it was love.

The oak bent down gently
With silver-leaved caress
And said to the small unicorn:

"My branches soar upwards
And spread out above you
Take refuge beneath these my wings;

Contradiction may shake thee
And sorrow o'ertake thee
But take courage thou child of light -

For naught lasts forever,
Nor the storm nor the sorrow,
And the earth is but fresher for rain."

To Virgil

Quando benigne tam otium datur et hora libenter,
    Quando tempus tam larga quam aqua mari,
Quando incipiet mens fieri turbida et vita odiosa,
    Inde, Virgile, tu – amator hominum et
Deum: poeta – ferens verba nobilia venis.
    Verba, confirment, fortia aesculus tam:
Auxilium dant per angustias perseverandum;
    Alta tam stella, alta tam mare:
Pingent significationeque colore saecula,
    Altior erigent, mentes illuminant,
Veritatis splendore. Virgile, multa te debeo;
    Non remunerari, sed quid habeo do:
Animum et studium, obediens bene verbis.

When so liberally leisure is given, and so readily hours,
    When time is as plentiful as water in the sea,
When the mind begins to be restless and life boring,
    Then, Virgil, you – lover of men and of gods:
Poet – you come bringing excellent words.
    Words, strong as the oak, they strengthen:
They give aid to persevere through difficulties;
    High as the stars, deep as the sea:
They paint the world with color and meaning;
    They raise up higher and illuminate minds
With the splendor of truth. Much do I owe you,
    Virgil; I cannot repay, but I give what I have:
Diligence, devotion, and good heeding of words.

Night Visitors

Through the balm of the air on a warm summer evening
When a hush over night-fall is peacefully weaving,
    The sharp raspy voices of crickets
    Chirp cheerfully out in the thickets,
But one, a bold wanderer, stops at my window,
    And takes up his violin bow;
In the darkling night crisply I hear it:
    Zeeezit, zeeezit.

The wind whispers a lullaby, rocking the treetops,
Telling softly of breezes that carry the raindrops;
    The cricket, I think, has gone on,
    Like a minstrel, still spreading his song;
Instead an audacious explorer in green
    Has come poking at my window-screen:
No night-sound has cicada for me,
    But in daylight: Zeezeeeee.

Fireworks

With thunderous sound the echoes roar,
          And deep the valley sings;
Unceasingly the rockets soar,
          And burst, and widely fling
Their bright star-show'rs and colored sparks
          And golden falling rain.
Their flashing light reveals in dark
          The smoke-trails of their train.

With BANG and POP are rent apart
          The heavens and the plains;
But BOOM will always throb your heart
          Like love or fear or pain.
The shaking of the earth and air,
          The echoes from afar,
The lights and sparks and smoke will fade;
          And only leave the stars.

Cygnet

Flying from the diving board
into the nine-foot pool,
Eyes full of elation,
repeat the round once more.

Boldly the little cygnet spreads
her moulting wings,
Scorning shallow water
to launch in the deep instead.

Startling the bird's awakening,
so shy she seemed;
Though so little knowing
so full of valiant daring.

Step from the edge, from the height,
glimpse the reflection—
Falling through water
is not so far from flight.

Love in Autumn

Delicate fingers in the night
caress my cheeks,
with butterfly touch you
brush the unkempt wisps of hair
that fall
over my tired face
aside.
You kissed my forehead
and my lips,
sang to me in a whisper
till I fell asleep.
O Wind,
I woke in the morning
to find you wept—
the golden leaves fall now
out of sight—
I feel them in
the chill fingers
you press
against my face.

Jack Frost

In
he creeps
on soft feet
through nooks, and crannies, and cracks,
but the old sun burns
on the hearth at home,
to shut him out
for a bit.

In
he comes
with strong strides
with the hale old ent-like man
when the door swings wide
to let him in. Outside
he paints
in soft brushstrokes, silver and white,
the window-glass;

Inside,
he nips the nose
of the fat white cat,
sends her scurrying to the stove
stepping in puddles of ice,
shaking her offended paws
in distaste;
she frowns
in displeasure,
with laid-back ears,
glares
with great gold eyes
at the sharp intruder
till the door is shut.

The old man chuckles,
“Don't sit so close
to the stove, Miss Puss,
you'll singe your whiskers,
and your long white fluff.”

“My fluff indeed,”
through narrowed eyes,
“no fear of that
since you
so kindly ask
old Jack Frost in, sir.”

Eileithyia & the Phoenix

Tumbling out into the light,
blinded,
like the night-owl
venturing into day
from the dark, sepulchral cave—
plunged by almighty hands
through storms and gushing rain,
and the ice-encrusted lake,
with stinging eyes squeezed shut,
not yet to see the shore
and the green shoots springing
into life—
baptized by water,
fire and night,
by blood and tears,
and last,
by light.

Pastoral

I Philomel spread out in the long grass
lying in the green pastures upon ancient hills
watch the sky dome flow over me like water.
My pipe lies idle in my out-flung hand;
my song has fled into the woods—
the birds sing it; the wind whispers it;
it is heavy in the drip of morning dew;
it streams through the colors of the sun's rising
but it breaks in the glory of the day's ending.
My verse blossomed in the new buds of spring,
and flourished in the summer woodlands' green,
danced with the sunset leaves of autumn,
and hid in the dry roots and branches
in winter under the bright silent snow.
Here outside of time, and in all times
I rest, feeling the press of hard ground amid
the meadow's conversation with the wind
whose light speech swirls the green fronds softly.
Sudden the nation's eagle whirls above me,
wingfeathers touched with sunlight
feeling the strength of the wind—the cold wind
lifting it high on powerful pinions—
and the last warmth of the day-dying sun
in a world frost-filled and glittering with snow.
Casting its keen eyes over the world
the noble bird moves among crimson clouds
both in and out of its own element—
such am I, the watcher, the piper fallen into silence.
Its soaring against the scattered stars
wakes me in a wonder without words
for flight in the light and the dark and the breeze
in the moving sky that is always changing.

Golden Years

Like gold fall the leaves
Of the latter days,
For the old world is fading
Away.

And some that turned brown
Were gathered and bound
Between leather and illumined
With gold.

Still a few on the boughs
Hang scarlet and orange,
Their fire still burns in
Your eyes.

But the wind is a-blowing;
The birds from the north
Like the years are all flying
Away.

I gather the geese
From the air with my eyes,
With my fingers the leaves
That are gold;

In words and in writing
I leave them for you:
The leaves that remain
Of years

That are gold.

Illumination

BANG!
purple and yellow pansies
make a statement
to the eyes:
neat rows of Indian ink,
thick curves in gold
and violet
amid a lot of green filigree
accented with white.
Illumination—
spring sun casting crimson
setting in the background;
remember the silver:
feathery expansions
of the mind—where you will,
but first,
follow the forms.

Quomodo sedet sola civitas . . .

How lonely sits the city—the city?
No, for she wanders, clothed in the mourning
black of a long trench-coat and tall boots
and a newsboy cap – all black –
pulled low against the misting rain,
and her eyes down-cast watch
the silver hoarfrost gather
in the black folds and fibers.

She was a bride once,
and once also a mother:
children ran through her houses and her streets
rang with their laughter,
and when war came, and famine
she fed them
till her own breasts ran dry and they left her—

She sent them.
Kindling a light which she gave them,
out into far and scattered places.
She herself now only what they are
and were and carry with them.
She herself as she is only
the shell of a woman in mourning.
She herself the desolate city,
silver dust lining the ledges.

She stops—bare budding trees reflecting
in shimmering water mirrors.

Bluebonnet Requiem

Walk with me beneath the trees
Just barely budding,
Now the sap is running.

Look one last time at the stone set
For a lost child long ago.

The snowflakes that still are falling,
White blossoms in time,
Quanah's sacrificial ashes
Blooming along roadsides, sown
By She-Who-Is-Alone.

Turn back and say goodbye
While time remains;

In season of scattered ashes
When this flower finally fades and falls,
We'll not regret, if we've loved.

Emotion, the Child

Sometimes people try to
analyze you,
tear you to shreds, ask why you
feel what you do
There is no
why for
it, wherefore
it -- it's a feeling, a song,
a poem, a child, a difficult toddler,
to be felt, loved, cherished, protected, and guided
to growth, not turned into
logical, cynical, rational, practical
arguments made of
limited, unfeeling
cold, hard, irritating
Words.
Wrap her up, the child, the toddler, the feeling
in a blanket, and hold her
gently,
Offer to make tea:
Let her exist as a child
in the space of pain,
so
She can be one
in spaces of joy.

Spun Life

The Spinner of Fates, seated
before the wide-spread tapestry
of this life, this world, this time
untangles fine, knotted, gnarled, torn,
broken threads from a minute weaving
within the whole
that belongs to me,
leaving a hole
She must re-spin, re-thread, re-make
Now, looks a long question at me:

Why are you so involved
so long, so often, so repeatedly,
with that silly investment banker
who cries,

"What other people have
is spun gold, and silver, and softest silk!
'Tis worth your change
more, oh, so much more,
than these here muted threads of yours.
Buy them, dye them, try them,
Make strange change for them."
Claims great fame in them.

And with musical lilt and coaxing words
most often
Sells stolen wares,
Asks finance for laundering,
Collects debts you do not owe.
Honesty's not his forté.

He knows his wares, I grant, at times
they are very good, at times worth a little
Investment -- a little, mind. At times,
they will return, but,
Beware, change not all
your own threads for his gilded ones.
Their quality declines. They break, knot,
and will not stretch to fit the space
You are, the space
You fill, the space
You grow into.

And when you try
to change all that is yours for his
well, see --
Here we are now, unravelling,
untangling
You.

November Mood

The leaves are falling
      from the red-gold trees.
I must teach you to write,
      when I hardly know how.
I must teach you patience
      through the winter into
Spring, but I'm impatient too.
   I must
show you healing
            when I'm broken
                  too.

All the leaves are falling,
      and the sky is gray.
You are disappointed,
      because you cared to
Hope—
      perhaps too much.
I am tired and sighing,
      because I tried to
Love—
      perhaps too much.

We are all falling
      in this autumn of the year.
We are all lost and breaking
      until spring.
We are all hibernating,
      enduring the days of short light
and long and longer darkness.

I will teach you to write,
if I have to teach myself
first, again, with love.
I will show you healing,
if I have to show myself
first, with infinite patience,

waiting for spring.

Picking up Patterns

I'm fairly good
at picking up patterns,
I suppose.

The rabbit jumps
from hole to hole,
disappears,
and surfaces again.

The frog from one
lily-pad to another
makes his way
unpredictably.

The little neurons in
your brain run wild
here and there
from one joy
to another enthusiasm
to a new curiosity.

I carefully pick
up all the threads
of the same
color and sort them
into piles.

Then deftly weaving them
together,
I tease out, ever so gently
the picture
they show me of you.

www.ingramcontent.com/pod-product-compliance
Lightning Source LLC
Chambersburg PA
CBHW051755130826
49812CB00033B/1167